Spanglibonics

iro

For Taylor's Fifth Birthday

gazing

Each
when separated
by the wind
become as insignificant
as the whole.
Yet we are compelled to adore it.
It is the blur between stripes
The Fajardo in its stitches. A matte
sun sitting there in the center of it all
offset and still shining over the blue.
Almost a reflection of the sea - superimposed onto
itself
when it waves in the wind. It is more akin to the
description of a cemi.
El Yunque in its blue corners fold
like the people do there. No statehood
or freedom song notes between these bars.
Just one star and not a state for it to stand.
Insignificant as the barely visible
loose thread
Until we finally
gaze close
enough.

these days

Woman smiling
– screaming waving
the flag
hips shake
the rhythms
into the sidewalks.
more skin
than cloth
raunch thrives
exploited bodies
all stick together.
sex staple
– the rewrite
pages say Manipulative
with a focus on
fabrication over
experience...

Being Híbrido

this   mundo

es   simple

pero   complex

y   split

como   identity

Ancestral Revive

During the search for Taino:

contemplation splits the spine,

hearts merge into shreds.

tonsils rip the sound barrier,

and we stumble upon being Latino.

Imperial Expectations

You want authenticity:
but djembe beating and do rags won't cut it.

You tell me to feel free:
but to scratch the black power fists.

After all there's only one star on my flag:
and some New York in the mix.

click-clack

With questions about self
we write for hours
across the spectrum
light, all colors - cultures
tell nothing of us
                scholars of our future
                    dig into the past
                searchin' for something
                pre-Columbian to grip
            grasp **click-clack** in place
    we have no story to tell our kids
            except the one we create
        and we know better than to lie
                        so we continue to seek
                        beyond beyond
                stuck in finite boxes we search the
                realms boxed in infinity

Continent Sized

To feel mountainous
Spread across the map like that
I'm continent sized

You are ocean
filling valleys
this topography is
nothing without your depth
you break me d o w n

I reach deeper
get close to your core to
dig in and flow between
rib caged indents and
overbitten fingernails

A Dali-tattooed back
round brown face
hiding under pink blush
heavy dimples smiling

the whole time
chipping away at
my earthquake zone to
force shatter between plates

You make my world split in two

One for me

One for you

First Time

My nerves tore from my limbs.
The cartilage shook salsa rhythms
and my hips followed hers.
I was lead into a taboo
anti-patriarchal swing.

As we swung
we soared into
A new masculinity.
The social constructs
around us
disappeared
while we explored
each other's circadian rhythms.
We synchronized.
          carried each other
through her living room.
I was scared.
She knew what to do.
She always does.

NYC Trains

The influencers lobby long
hours for:
black babies screaming
overhead and white babies
being caressed:
loved so well.

We're taught to exploit each other
via ingestion without question:
twerking to our phones
criticizing each other and
ignoring the superstructures
at play.

We walk with masculinity
on high and
respect for women on low.

Machismo in our
back pocket:
we're masked
trapped in our heads.

A combo leading to
cognitive dissonance
louder than our traditions.

We all have trouble disproving:
the deeply ingrained.
If the result is
depicted well,
can you really blame us?

Color

she paints like jazz

painted finger stroke

sponge twists and

two steps with

paint rolled on the side

of a pencil

Process

dab swipe wipe
clean dirty
mix and mingle
these colors
swing and jar
ajar from their jar
to the pallet
onto the floor
the stain that
turned into a
masterpiece

Scraping the Sky

scrape

the utensils
on canvas
tear at our stories

scr ap e
textures are rhythms
unknown to our consciousness
so we sink into overlap
trial and error

s   c   r   a   p   e

reflections cluster at
the thought of
being so close
to the clouds under us

s   c   a   e

Gravestones

Gravestones - got minds of their own.

Funerals cost so much that
we stack wills against 'em.

We wonder how people don't feel
the need - to worry about death.

Seen many funerals - stopped so many attempts.

We stay hyper-cognizant
of our options
so we go the other route - instead of lock up or
boxin'

Wind tunnels blow - silent fire - south

Left with no choice - Like everyone - else.

Mourning

through
the morning,
until the night -
meets the Sun.
When the day breaks
us fast -
into tomorrow.
We hold each other -
Brothers.
As if what's
in front of us,
isn't surreal.

Letter from a Blind Couple

Dear Young Lovers
You know little of this
sparkle under our skin.
We've learned to see
each other through
our fingertips.
We caress with the only eyes we've
been given - fingernails mapping
each other's physical frame
out in four dimensions.

Tell each other how much
we love the way we look at
each other while
holding our chests
close enough to see the
movement in our ribcages.
You cannot imagine the intensity
we feel when our bodies become one,
when we dance with all of the
lights off and see everything.

You Know Them

Those people
who are at
the cusp of
being in your
life.

The trapeze artists
balancing
on your
aspirations?

Yeah.
Them.

Poencetry

I can't dance so
I write you a poence

To show you the stride
In my lines

The pep in my step and
the groove in my literary tools

All these hearts

all these Hearts
and no love.
a world where
Hearts are sold and
given as gifts.
chocolate filling
and saints and babies
with wings and
no pants.

all these Hearts
and no love.

Fingers in my brain

the scholars of the past
                    while I scribe
focus on the future
with the fingers from the past
kneading the cells in my cerebellum

                                        must cite

                    must cite
must cite the past while digging into the future
the future in site

                                                cite

cite for future sight
being a visionary is a pain in the brain
    they keep poking me - these scholars of the past
their intellectual indexes tickling the inside of my
forehead
you can see their knuckles

                                in place of my veins
calloused insides sore from this massage
                    this message

                                        massage

message that massages my creativity
makes me want to fight-write, write less than more
strive to be innovative but rubbed into a trance
trance-like state
                        wait

                                        weight

weighing me down
there's no way i can be as intellectual as them
                    every idea already written
                            already told, explored and presented
i am no clone

they want me to be a
                    drone of Intel
a WASP reincarnated as a wasp-drone.
drone   done   drone
         done.
                                              done.

Entrapment

Afro-Latino
Boricua mistaken for
Filipino
With aligned histories
In our lost memory bank.

Rarely retrieved but when
It is, we scream pride
And joy. We love our
Brothers but draw the line
So we don't get too close.

Afraid to be marked by masculine-taboos
Instead of simply practicing free love
Namaste comes to mind with
all of my faculties in free play.

Stockholm syndrome with myself
My other conscience array
Genetics of gorgeous –
No rational interruption
We need two kids & a wife to be
Regarded as proper.

There is no room for us
in these complex cities.

Difference

original
with no origins
we strive to be
too much of us
not enough of each other
at the same time
we fail to see
the connected
ness

Open Palm

My dream is to one day
-with an open palm-
Summon your participation.
I'll lead and
you'll just follow.
You'll cum at my ability to
lead you through each note.
Each hip sway will clear a
Shortcoming of mine.
Every proper step will
make you blush with pride

Termites to the Soul

Our deepest feelings will
tear away at our guts
like termites to the soul
we'll feel them eating us
from the inside out.

The population will fluctuate.

Some days the numbers will be low
but in those moments
when your body eats itself
from the inside out
remember you are
worthy of being eaten in the first place.

Superhuman Nights

Dreamt myself into my son's imagination.
I turn pillow into skyscraper my
sheets into sky & six into spidey.
Make my skin scale red and blue.

I turn pillow into skyscraper my
mind, becomes my wish.
Sheets into sky and six into spidey.
He'll never believe how this

mind becomes my wish.
In dreams, I'm my son's favorite superhero.
He'll never believe how this
sticky soled individual saves folks.

My subconscious saves us.
Sheet into sky & six into spidey.
The things I'd do to be better for my boy, I even
Dreamt myself into my son's imagination.

One Day

Brown dimples being created
by my shoulder blades
pressed against her cheeks.

Her warmth carrying itself
through the sheets while
I grip her absence.

The reflection of the
almond in her eyes flickering
above my windowsill.

The fibers of her being
whispering
exhales of affection.

One day she won't have to leave.

iro

Artists' Grind

The Power:

Behind dark corners of the body.
In the form and physique that isn't
about the performance.

The Ability:

To adhere to expectations while
twisting and turning the abstract
to make it seem norm.
The making it all seem norm.

The Strength:

Form
and physique.
Sitting down sometimes
but never taking a knee.
Covering the realities
of this story two-fold.

The Focus:

Half smile and cutthroat.
Never taking a knee
Open palms and exposed sole.
The two-tone.

The Story:

Beauty placed in front of the flex.
The two-toned flex.
Less being more.
Careful code-switch.
The seemingly depicted
but left untold.

SPANGLIBONICS

ABOUT THE AUTHOR

Carlos iro Burgos, a Bronx, NY native who spent most of his life in Yonkers, NY, is a father, avid questioner of masculinities, and explorer of identity. iro's first poetry collection, From Boy to IRO is used throughout The City University of NY as required text in Puerto Rican History and Culture courses and in other classes within the system as supplementary texts. His newest work, Spanglibonics, explores the experiences of Afro-Nuyoricans through emotionally driven, vulnerable poetry that demands openness to new ways of thinking about the world.

Over the years, iro has served as a judge, and sometimes host, for Global Writes, Inc.'s slam poetry competitions at Lehman College and currently serves on the organization's Board of Directors. iro has performed at venues such as the Schomburg Theater in Harlem, Bowery Poetry Club, El Museo del Barrio, Iona College, Clark Atlanta University and the legendary Nuyorican Poet's Café. iro has also co-written two professional plays that toured the national college circuit.

iro holds an M.S.Ed. in Higher Education from the University of Pennsylvania's Graduate School of Education and a B.A. in English Creative Writing from Hunter College, City University of New York.

Made in the USA
Middletown, DE
26 April 2018